THE POWER THAT WORKS

Infinite Power, Infinite Possibilities

CHRIS GBENLE

CGB
PUBLISHING
SCOTLAND

THE POWER THAT WORKS
Infinite Power, Infinite Possibilities

Chris Gbenle

Published by **CGB Publishing** Scotland

First published 2025

ISBN: 978-1-9996053-4-6

Cover Design/layout: Imaginovation Ltd.

Printed in the United Kingdom.

CONTENTS

Now to him who is able to do immeasurably more than all we ask or imagine, according to ***his power that is at work within us***

(Ephesians 3:20 NIV)

DEDICATION

This book is dedicated to my beloved sister who has been a constant feature in my life until less than a year ago, when you had to go home to your creator and Lord.

You always celebrate me, I believe you will be cheering me on now as part of the cloud of witnesses.

You are sorely missed, Ashake, my dear sister.

FOREWORD

In a world where we often find ourselves grappling with uncertainty and turmoil, the undeniable presence of God's power serves as a beacon of hope and strength. "The Power That Works" invites readers to embark on a transformative journey through the diverse dimensions of God's power, illuminating how His might not only shapes our lives but also guides us, blesses us, corrects us, and renews our spirits.

This book stands as a testament to the unfathomable greatness of God, exploring the profound truths found in Scripture and the guiding presence of the Holy Spirit. Each chapter reveals the multifaceted ways in which God's power operates in our lives—from offering us direction in times of confusion to pouring out blessings that elevate our spirits and circumstances.

As we delve deeper into the themes presented in this book, we will come to understand that God's power is not merely a distant force; it is an intimate, active presence that desires to engage with us. It brings healing to our souls, renews our minds, and shapes our hearts, preparing us to fulfil the purpose for which we were created.

I encourage you to approach the pages of this book with an open heart and a willing spirit. Allow the words within to challenge, inspire, and transform you. As you discover the magnificent power of God at work in every aspect of your life, may you find renewed strength, unwavering faith, and a deeper relationship with the One who is able to do immeasurably more than we ask or imagine.

May this book empower you to embrace the abundant life that God has promised—a life rich in purpose and filled with His extraordinary grace.

Blessings,
Pastor Leke Sanusi
Continental Overseer,
The Redeemed Christian Church of God
Europe Continent 9

PREFACE

The universal currency of transaction is power. Every transaction that goes on either in heaven or here on earth is an interplay of power. As a matter of fact, the knowledge of who you are as a person is measured by the quantity of power you possess. Power is wealth, which can be in form of spiritual, material, intellectual, emotional or political power.

Nature also teaches us that power is an indispensable part of our lives. At birth, for instance, the first thing that birth attendants look out for when a child is born is whether or not that child has enough strength in him/her to start life and live. Once they see the signs of strength in a child, only then will the rejoicing begin. The very first sign of strength that is easily observable is the loud cry of a newborn. At the other extreme is the fact that at the moment of exit from this world, there is a vanishing of the power of life.

So, what these illustrations tell us is that our lives circle around power. We cannot run away from this reality.

In Luke 11:21-22, the Lord Jesus Christ said that the differentiating mark between a conquered person and his conqueror is the degree of power that each of them possesses. He said when a strong man who is fully armed guards his own palace, his goods are in peace. But then, He quickly established that a more powerful person can dispossess the one who has hitherto been lauded as strong and brave.

It is a world of power, and you only need to have been around for a few years to understand this fact. The people you meet out there on the street who speak with so much confidence and authority do so because there is a certain degree of power that they have anchored their lives on that fuels their audacity. Some careless persons have ignorantly dared the threats and pronouncements of other men, and the story did not end well. It takes a greater power, the power of God, to confront the powers of the world regardless of their degree of potency. There are many issues that we throw intellectual energy and money into, while all we need to do is to approach the Source of all powers, to experience deliverance and comprehensive victory.

That great power we mentioned earlier, is one that God had purposed from the very foundation of the world to make known to the world. Taking a trip back to the exodus of the children of Israel from Egypt (Exodus 9:16), God declared expressly to Moses that He designed the occasion just to reveal His power and so that His name will be publicized across the earth. That is power!

There are gradations of power. There are people who have the power to deny you funds, there are people who have the power to deny you accommodation, there are people who have the power to deny you employment, and interestingly, our Lord Jesus Christ said there are people who have the power to kill the body, but that is the limit of all physical powers. Jesus said regardless of the degree of power people command, the only one we should fear is the One who has the power to both kill and cast into hell (Luke 12:5). And that is God!

The Christian faith and the world evangelization mission is also predicated on power. Acts 4:33 makes it sufficiently clear that the early witnesses, the apostles of our Lord Jesus Christ, gave witness to His resurrection with great power. It was that great power that defined the ministries of the early disciples, and it is still the separator today of those who will do great things in God and for God. I am convinced that you will like to be amongst those whose lives will be judged as impactful and impregnable.

ACKNOWLEDGEMENT

I am totally and perpetually indebted to my Lord and King, the source of my strength and the captain of my soul, the Lord Jesus Christ. By Your power, you made this nobody to be somebody in you. All my praise shall for all eternity be given to you, my Saviour.

I will like to specifically thank the team that worked with me on this project. The great effort of a dear disciple of Christ, Ayodeji Olonode who bought into the vision of publishing this book will forever be appreciated. And to the whole CGB Publishing team, thank you for being ever so reliable.

To my spiritual family in the Redeemed Christian Church of God worldwide and the United Kingdom, thank you for being to me what a good family is.

The Fountain of Love family, you are simply just the best. It's going on three decades together now, and it has just been a joy to grow together with you.

My most dear and respected leader, genuine beloved brother, Pastor Leke Sanusi, thank you so much for agreeing to write the foreword to this book. I am most honoured to be called your friend. I appreciate you greatly, sir.

My sincere appreciation to my dear wife, Pastor (Mrs.) Nike Gbenle for giving me a peaceful home where I could do what the Lord has called me to do. Our marriage and friendship of over three and half decades, blessed with the most wonderful children and grandchildren has been a major blessing. Thank you my dearest.

CHAPTER ONE

THE POWERLESS, THE EMPOWERED AND THE PURPOSE OF POWER

The Sad State of The Powerless

IT IS A sad thing to be powerless. Powerlessness is a state in which anyone can ride upon the one who is weak, anyone can step upon him and trample upon him.

The worst part of being powerless is that when the power is needed, the person does not have the needed power to execute his intentions or desires. The Prophet Isaiah, in Isaiah 37:3, described a pathetic scenario of a pregnant woman who came to the fullness of her term but lacked strength to travail and bring to birth the child she carried. Put differently, it is a shameful state where they knock on a person's door with high expectations and the person is unable to meet the expectations.

> Powerlessness is a sad state, and the people of the world are looking for the powerless to oppress, to dominate and tyrannize...

These things find expression even in everyday realities, instances like strategic conversations where a person is expected to come up with some wisdom that brings solutions but rather the contribution is weak and lacking in substance. Powerlessness is unattractive. Powerlessness is a sad state, and the people of the world are looking for the powerless to oppress, to dominate and tyrannize until there is nothing left of the person.

Having said all, the main question remains, and that is: why are people powerless?

a. Supply Deficiency

One of the reasons why people are powerless is because the power is just not there (QED). No amount of talk can change the situation, the power is just not there. And if we examine our lives closely, we are likely to discover that we have all been there at some point or another in our journey. Matthew 17:14-19 presents a pitiable experience that the disciples of Jesus had; a day when they almost became public spectacles. They were practically helpless when a man brought his son who suffered seizures because an unclean spirit was bent on destroying him completely by throwing him into fire or water. You can imagine how sorrowful the disciples were on that day, because verse 19 recorded that they came back to the Master to ask why they were not equal to the task. The response Jesus gave was more like "the deposit of power in your life is not enough for the job, you need to access power through prayer and fasting..." In Luke 24:49, Jesus gave them a warning when He was leaving; He warned them to temper their zeal for witnessing until they had been endued with power from on high. They were wise enough to lay hold of power before swinging into action. Conversely, Acts 19:14-17 recorded for us the experience of some charlatans popularly known as the sons of Sceva, who were supply deficient yet decided to put up a front (forgetting that power is not just in words, but in action). Nothing is more shameful than when people expect you to deliver but you cannot.

b. Sensibility Deficiency

There are people who have power, who carry a measure influence and control but lack an awareness of what they have. Judges 6:12-16 gives us an example of someone who walked in this reality – Gideon. The man had a response to everything the Angel that appeared to him had to say concerning him, but thank God for the grace that was sufficient to pull him through his lack of awareness. As a child of God, as one whose sins are forgiven and has yielded to the Lordship of Jesus Christ, there is a power deposit in you that is greater than the powers of the world. Don't fret at the threat of unreasonable men, you are more than what is visible to the eyes.

c. Sustainability Deficiency

Sustainability deficiency means that you have the power but it has been leaking, and the day when it is required, such a person may not be able to deliver. Judges 16:20-22 speaks about an anointed man called Samson, who suffered leakage of power. One day, he rose up like he was accustomed to doing, but the difference was that on this particular day, the power had left him and he did not realize it. Some people find themselves in similar situation, where things they consider easy and straightforward have turned out to cause an upset or embarrassing moment for them because the grace that made it easy yesterday has departed from them without them realizing it.

The Sure Status of The Empowered

How do we become empowered?

a. Recognize your need for power (no hubris, no excuses).

Know your limit, know the extent to which available resources (in terms of power) can carry you. If you are not equipped for a task, there is no need for bravado. Humble yourself and recognize your need for power. One of the most dangerous creeds flying about today is the philosophy of "fake it till you make it". That is a very dangerous and unscriptural stance. Why fake it when you can easily go to God whose resources are inexhaustible. James 1:5 says the one who needs wisdom should ask God who gives generously to all men. Only fools do not recognize their need for what they need.

b. Evaluate where you are.

Carry out regular self-assessments according to II Corinthians 13:5, so as to know where you stand in the now. Luke 14:28-33 emphasized the importance of evaluation when it clearly states that a person who is commencing a project must be careful to count the cost of the project vis-à-vis the resources available so that it does not become a misadventure in the end. Evaluate where you are, and that cuts across every area of life: your spiritual life, prayer life, fasting life, study of the Word, your relationship with key people in your life, and your followership of Jesus. Your evaluation should not be based on what men think about you because their views may vary based on their mood. People may project you far above the level that you actually are. You know more about yourself more than others can tell you, and that is why self-assessment is important. But above all, let God mark your scripts because He alone knew us ever before we were formed in the womb. Approach Him prayerfully asking Him to show you where you stand in the scheme of things.

c. **Seek to be empowered.**

Great people are seekers of great things. If a person is not hungry, not thirsty, not desperate enough, such a person can never be empowered. Thrusting power to a careless person who probably does not value it or not aware of his need for it is like casting pearls before swine; they will trample them under feet and rend the giver to pieces (Matthew 7:6). The Apostle Paul was one great example of someone who sought great things – he sought the knowledge of God and the full accompaniments that comes with that knowledge. He said 'that I may know Him and the power of His resurrection...' Despite all the exploits, he still had a very palpable hunger, he continued to press on, he judged himself as having not attained, he wanted more!

d. Pursue wisdom.

The only way to keep power and use it well is through wisdom. According to a nineteenth century English historian, Lord Acton, *power tends to corrupt and absolute power corrupts absolutely*; and when something is corrupted, it has to be discarded because it is of no use any more. So, a sightless seeking of power will end in no good. This explains why the man called Solomon, the wisest in his days, described wisdom as the principal thing (Proverbs

4:7), adding that in all of man's getting, there is need to get understanding. Seek power, but also seek wisdom because a foolish man with material power will soon go penniless (Proverbs 21:20). Leaders of nations and establishments have gotten into trouble with the law because they could not balance power with wisdom. Examples abound of people who evidently possessed spiritual power but lacked discretion and this became their undoing. Some became proud, some became reckless and could not rein themselves in, and the story just did not end well for such people. The nuance that separates powerful people from the pack, is wisdom. There are many powerful people in the world today by different parameters, but wisdom stands the real men out. Wisdom provides a compass for vigilant navigation through the terrain of power. It is possible to be powerful and no other department of your life suffers for it, but that is only possible when wisdom is in the mix.

Wisdom provides a compass for vigilant navigation through the terrain of power.

Many have gotten power but to the ruin of their family and precious relationships.

The Purpose of Power

All power belong to God, and everyone must account for the power given to him/her (Romans 14:12, Matthew 5:14-30). Therefore, power must be used to:

a. **Glorify God.**

   An acknowledgement of the fact that all power derives from God is the first step to glorifying God. Living our lives with the consciousness of bringing pleasure to the heart of God through the way we use the power we possess or the resources at our disposal is a great step to glorifying God. Any power that you possess that does not glorify God, any power that you possess that makes you assume 'God status' over your affairs or the affairs of other men is a very dangerous power.

b. **Help others and make the goodness of God known.**

   We are empowered to add value to other people

and by extension improve our communities. It is through such expressions that God is glorified. Any power we receive that does not benefit our neighbours, or that does not benefit people around us, is a power we must be wary of.

c. **Show the world how good God is.**

From the story of the children of Israel, every form of display of power that was recorded right from Egypt till they sojourned in the wilderness was a show of the goodness of God to His own chosen people. The nations around heard about it and they paid close attention to the God of Israel. Even the ones that tried to defy them also became study cases of how powerful the God of Israel is.

d. **Resist evil and establish righteousness.**

Jesus Christ Himself was revealed for the purpose of destroying the works of the devil. He came to spoil principalities, powers, rulers of darkness and every named hierarchy of evil, to the end that righteousness be established and God the Father be glorified. Acts 8:8 gave us the example of a young man called Phillip, who went to Samaria in the power of the Holy Ghost, ministered the work, cast out demons and caused great joy to erupt in the city. That is the purpose of power.

CHAPTER TWO

THE GREAT POWER OF GOD

Ah, Lord GOD! Behold, You have made the heaven and the earth ***by Your great power and outstretched arm, and there is nothing too hard for You***
(Jeremiah 32:17, NKJV)

WE CANNOT OVEREMPHASIZE the fact that the cosmic currency of transaction is power. In every realm of existence, the real currency of transaction is power. That is why it is better to possess power, else a person may not stand any chance of survival. The lion wakes up every morning with only one goal in mind – that it won't go hungry that day.

The antelope, for instance, also wakes up with the determination that it won't become a prey to any predator. The goal of staying fed and the determination to survive both come down to the amount of power each creature possesses to propel it through each day. As we must have read earlier, a powerless life is a painful and frustrating life.

...There is absolutely no power (in any known form) especially in men's realm that does not derive its source ultimately from God.

Now, it is important to establish that God rules in the affairs of men (Daniel 4:17). Therefore, as much as power is the cosmic currency of transaction, there is absolutely no power (in any known form) especially in men's realm that does not derive its source ultimately from God. In Deuteronomy 8:18, the scripture gives an example of how God cautioned the people of Israel that after they had gotten settled in their own land and had become prosperous, they should be careful not to attribute the power that produced the wealth to their physical, mental or even economic abilities.

Rather, He admonished them to remember always that the power to make wealth comes from God. And just in case anyone thinks this admonition is only applicable only to the people of God, cast your mind back to Nebuchadnezzar, the Babylonian king who thought the greatness of the empire (which was the world power at that time) was by his administrative and military aptitude. God had to remind him who truly owns all power (Daniel 4:30-33). God is great in power!

Our Lord Jesus Christ, who was the express image of the invisible God gave us a sneak-peek into the greatness of God's power with His terrific interventions in men's affairs while He walked upon the earth. Luke 5:17 tells us that on one occasion, while He was simply teaching and exhorting the people who gathered unto Him, the power of God was present to heal the people. Power is only as good as the use to which you put it. So, we need to be very sure that the power of God at our disposal or the power of God we so desire to see at work in us, is well defined as to its scope and its potency. A person holding a gun, for instance, and does not know what the gun can do is as useless as one who does not have it. And that is why it is expedient to understand the dimensions and areas of deployment of God's great power.

What can the power of God do?

a. **Power to Save (The power of God is manifested in salvation of souls)**

Most believers tend to get worried when people around them are not getting saved, but the truth is that if it depends on you, we ourselves would not have been saved. Nobody can teach you to be saved because the salvation of God is a mystery and that mystery is rooted in the power of God that changes a person's desire and appetite. The Psalmist in Psalms 106:8 established one important fact about the potency of God's power. He said:

Nevertheless He saved them for his name's sake, that He might make his mighty power to be known.

There is nothing that displays the power of God more than the salvation of the souls of men.

b. Power to Deliver

Never ever let anyone threaten you when you are certain you are doing the will of God. As long as you are in the will of God, He is able to deliver you from the assault of wicked men. The example of the arrogant king called Sennacherib should give us an idea of God's power to deliver. He threatened the people of God and even dared their God to deliver them from his hands, but it took just one Angel to settle the matter (II Kings 18:17-19:37). What about David? His encounter with Goliath who threatened the children of Israel for 40 days nonstop (as well as David's previous encounters with a lion and a bear) were other examples of the power of God to deliver us from threats to our lives (I Samuel 17:1-51).

c. Power to Heal

God is a Healer. Again, Jesus Christ, the visible image of the invisible God, proved this during His earthly ministry because the Bible recorded that He went about doing good and healing all those who were oppressed (Acts 10:38). Do we advise people not to visit the hospital? Definitely not, because

God uses the skills and knowledge of medical professionals to keep people in good state of health. But we must realize that except the Lord builds the house, in vain is the labour of the builders (Psalms 127:1). Everyone in medical practice or healthcare profession are at best caregivers (caring at different levels and getting paid different salaries for caring in different ways or areas of specialization). The power to heal ultimately comes from God.

...Only God has the authority to go by the name 'Healer'.

d. Power to Bless

This is one area we must pay close attention to. To start with, blessing is when all power in all realms of existence are summoned to assist and work in favour of a person. This explains why even the errors of a blessed person appears novel or like an invention sometimes; because everything just appears to work in their favour. A curse is just the direct opposite of this expression – every power in every realm of existence are summoned to work against a person. We must be careful to understand that the power to bless resides primarily with God, and He demonstrated that right from Genesis 1:28, after He had made man, the very first thing He did was to pronounce a blessing. We must make it a personal quest to seek the blessings of God every day of our lives, either directly from the mouth of God or from those who act as proxies – parents, spouses, authority figures, spiritual leaders and genuine brethren. God in His mercy and sovereignty has instituted proxies among men who have the power to bless, like the example of Aaron and his sons whom the Lord authorized to bless the people of God in Numbers 6:24-26. The power in the blessing of God is so great that no degree of sorcery or enchantment or divination can withstand it. A man like Balaam was definitely not one to toy with, a man whose divination was so great that he undulates between righteous and unrighteous. Balak, king of Moab, was so sure that if only Balaam could place a curse on the people of God, they would become easy preys to the Moabites. But sacrifice upon sacrifice, enchantment upon enchantment, Balaam came to the conclusion that those whom God had not cursed cannot be cursed by any man (Numbers 23:13-23). Such is the power of God's blessing.

e. Power to Make Fruitful

The power of increase resides with God. The Apostle Paul testified of this in I Corinthians 3:6 that even though he ensures he was diligent in planting and Apollos manages the irrigation part of the process, the One who really brings the increase is God. One major sign of a curse is labouring without results: an evidence that the earth is not yielding its fruit for a man – it is a very terrible position to be in. Fruitless labour is antithetical to who God is. You can begin to put a context to the episode recorded in Mark 11:12-14, 20-21, with the fig tree that was not bearing fruit according to the expectations of the Master. God is not just deeply interested in the harvest but in the entire cycle of fruitfulness which begins with having a seed to plant. When a man does not have seed to

One major sign of a curse is labouring without results...

plant, the important step for him to take at that point in time is to turn to God who gives seed to the sower (II Corinthians 9:10). There is another possibility, which is that a person may have the seed to plant but the ground is hard – a contentious environment, a toxic environment and generally speaking, an environment that is not just right for performance. But God promised in Jeremiah 23:29 that His Word is like the hammer that is able to break rocks in pieces. Another possibility is that there may be seed, the ground may be good, but there is no rain to irrigate the ground; but the interesting thing is that God has absolute control over rain and He is able to pour it on our ground in abundance (Isaiah 55:10-11, Isaiah 44:3). Another possibility is that there may be seed, the ground may be good and well irrigated, but then there are wasters who come in to destroy the harvest – locusts, termites, caterpillars, cankerworms, etc. Locusts come suddenly (like an infestation), but termites are elements that are resident in the system to cause a leak. When a person is doing business and it always results in losses, or when a person decides to invest in a sector, and the market slumps after he has invested, that is the activities of wasters at work. However, in whatever form these wasters operate, the power of God is able to take care of them.

CHAPTER THREE

THE POWER OF GUIDANCE

A BLESSED PERSON is known by the abundance of help he/she receives. It was recorded in scriptures that Uzzah, one of the kings in Israel was a man marvelously helped by God. (II Chronicles 26: 15) That particular statement made him to stand out in the sense that he did what no other king in Israel did and we can boldly say that no other person did it in the Bible. He was the man who introduced technology into warfare. It takes God's help to have a man come up with such towering invention.

To stand out in your generation, God must help you. But just in case you are imagining and wondering about those who do not believe in God, yet things are going well for them, remember that God rules in the affairs of men and no man should ever disparage or trivialize the help that comes from above - it is the major difference between success and failure. But of all the help that a person can receive, I believe that guidance is one of the greatest help that one can receive. In Isaiah 58:11, the Bible says:

To stand out in your generation, God must help you.

> *The Lord will guide you continually and satisfy your soul in drought and strengthen your bones; you shall be like a watered garden and like a spring of water, whose waters do not fail.* (NKJV)

Some of the greatest prayers anyone can pray are: *"Help me O Lord!"* and *"Guide me O Lord!"*

The Scope of Guidance

An understanding of the ways in which God guides a person goes a long way in directing how such a person prays. So, what does guidance or being guided entail?

1. ***Guided away from danger***

   This expression of guidance was visible in the case of the king of Israel in II Kings 6:9, who had Elisha (a man who was in contact with God) providing guidance for him and the armies of Israel against the incessant battle arrays of the king of Syria. Not once, not twice were his feet directed away from danger until the matter became a cause for concern to the king of Syria and he began to suspect his officers of being fifth columnists in the army. Oh, how sweet it is for a person's life to be marked by divine guidance to the end that he does not fall into danger. Personally, one of the first signs that assured me that God has taken over my life was that I was no longer walking into danger. Another good example of guidance away from danger was seen in King David's life. According to II Samuel 17:21, during the Absalom rebellion, when Ahitophel, his personal counsellor had aligned with the rebellion and advised on how to kill David; but David was guided out of that dangerous plot through the help of God.

2. ***Guided out of danger***

There is another dimension of guidance as it relates with danger, and that is being guided out of a danger that we have already entered into, knowingly or unknowingly. King David found himself in a situation when he was practically in danger of being killed by a Philistine giant who was very close to striking David at a time when his reflexes were not as sharp as it used to be. It took one of His men to wade in to prevent that danger from overcoming David (II Samuel 21:15-17). There is no situation so dangerous that God cannot bring a person out from. Peter was another example of someone in a precarious place, having denied his Lord three times, but the Lord

There is a power that can guide a man out of danger, and that power resides in God alone.

brought him out from the danger of guilt and shame and made him the pillar of the early Church (John 21:15-19). There is a power that can guide a man out of danger, and that power resides in God alone.

3. *Guided into blessing*

People talk about finding themselves in the right place at the right time; that is an example of being guided into blessing. Such things do not occur by happenstance, it is the power of God that guides into blessings that account for such instances. In I Samuel 17:17, David had a firsthand experience of the working of this power. He was just meant to take some supplies to his brothers on the field, and that single trip was what cemented his kingship because that was the occasion when he killed Goliath and the attention of the people of Israel got drawn to him.

4. *Guided in the blessing*

God's guidance not only ushers a man into blessing but is also available to guide the person in the blessing so that he does not mess things up. One of the greatest pains of life is that some people stopped being guided in their blessings – they walked into the blessing but could not stand in the blessing. I Samuel 18:5 (and verses 14 and 30), after David walked into the blessing of killing Goliath and the fame and adulation that came with it, the Bible recorded that David continued to behave himself wisely. That is an example of being guided in blessing. There are very qualified people who have landed big opportunities but were never able to retain the opportunities, because for every step in the right direction there is the possibility of a misstep in the process. This is why we need to be guided in blessing.

The Necessity of Divine Guidance

We need God to guide us because:

1. ***We do not see far enough***. The fact that no man has precise and accurate knowledge of what will happen tomorrow gives credence to the fact that we do not see far enough and therefore need to be divinely guided by the One whose name is El-Roi,

the God who sees. No man can guarantee that what is there today will be there tomorrow. This explains why the author of Proverbs warned us not to lean on our own understanding but acknowledge God in all our ways and He will direct our path (Proverbs 3:5-6). All the permutations of this world cannot take a person far because they are based on conjectures and deductions, but God's guidance alone is what can take us far because it is based on eternal truth and reality.

2. ***We do not know well enough.*** There are many things we do not know about ourselves except God reveals them to us. How much more the things we do not know about the world we live in. That is why God said in Jeremiah 33:3 that when you call upon Him, He will not only answer but grant you an insight into great and mighty things that you do not know. This is what some people may choose to call 'insider information', because it is not common knowledge, it is not public knowledge, it is knowledge direct from the Source of all knowledge. This marks a big difference between lasting success and languishing.

3. ***We do not feel safe enough.*** We need divine guidance because we do not feel safe enough to step out, or put differently, we lack courage. Reading through Judges 6 and 7, it is quite surprising to know how feeble the man Gideon was despite the Angel proclaiming to him that he was a man of valour (a mighty man). Every step of the way, until he was able to stand on his feet and embrace the assignment he was called to, God was guiding him through the journey of self-discovery, the journey of courage and the journey of assurance. It was God's guidance that pulled him through to the point where he acquired sufficient confidence to lay hold on what God had in store for him.

4. ***We are not strong enough.*** Naturally speaking, the strongest of men is very feeble. One situation of life is enough to break a person and reduce him to shreds. But regardless of our feebleness, God through His guidance is able to move us forward even in the midst of adverse winds and other unpleasant conditions. The story of David in I Samuel 17 is instructive. Even Goliath,

David's opponent, knew that this was a very weak individual (humanly speaking). He felt deeply insulted that the best Israel could put forward was a young feeble guy who knows nothing about the art of war and this was validated by the fact that he approached a fully-armed warrior with a staff in his hand. But what Goliath did not see was the fact that David was guided by God throughout that process. The testimony he gave before Saul, the choice of weapons (five smooth stones and a sling), his rejection of the armour of Saul, the responses he gave to all of Goliath's threat, the timing of his attack, all proved that David was divinely guided. If God does not guide us, we are prone to crash because of our emotional and physical frailties. This explains why even in our times of prayer, the Spirit of God still guides us on how to pray because we do not know how to pray as we ought to (Romans 8:26).

5. ***We are not wise enough.*** This is where the issue of decision making comes in because we need the wisdom of God to be able to decide whether to go

right or to go left. Turning in the wrong direction is a very disastrous experience. It has cost men their hard-earned resources, it has cost some others irredeemable years, it has cost many others valuable relationships, and some others have had to pay the price with their lives.

How To Obtain Divine Guidance

The following are guidelines for being guided by God:

1. ***Be acquainted with the voice of God.*** If you must be guided by a person, you must know his voice. So, the starting point to obtaining divine guidance is knowing the voice of God, and part of the ways to get acquainted with the voice of God include:

    a. Know the Living Word (Hebrews 1:1-3). You cannot be guided at the highest level possible except you come to the knowledge of Jesus Christ. Of course, those that do not know Jesus occasionally get sparkles of guidance for the purpose of benefitting humanity, but that does not make them partakers of the divine nature yet, until they accept the Lordship of Jesus Christ and submit to Him completely. For a child of God, life goes beyond just having a rounded life, it is about eternal life and the starting point is knowing Jesus.

b. Study the Written Word. The written word of God serves a purpose because it reveals the speakings and the dealings of God to us. This is because the scriptures are written for our learning so that we can come to an understanding of how to conduct ourselves. The Bible is the believer's introduction to the voice of God, and any voice, speakings or dealings contrary to the scriptures is a red flag that we must be very careful.

c. Explore the various means of God's communication with you. God talks to individuals differently. For some people, it is by dreams, for some others, it is by impression. Some people are feelers, some are seers and some others are hearers. But it is important to understand how God talks to us as individuals.

2. ***Be acquainted with the ways of God***

   a. God is sovereign. When we talk of being guided by God, it means you must submit to His sovereignty because His methodology transcends our understanding and our ways are not His ways. Imagine the story in I Kings 19:9-15, when God decided to meet Elijah's needs in an unusual way - making him drink from a brook and commanding ravens to bring food to him. Along the line the formula changed, the brook dried up and the ravens stopped bringing supplies because God had prepared another channel, a widow (a widow who had just one meal left and was hoping to have a sad last supper with her son). I believe it must have been some mental struggle for Elijah, but he knew the almightiness and sovereignty of God. If you can acquaint yourself with God's ways, especially His sovereignty, He can guide you in ways that may seem foolish by human standards but that will birth miraculous occurrences in your life. The fact that God moves pieces around does not make Him haphazard. You just need to trust in His sovereignty (Psalms 115:3) and His sovereignty will birth His purposes in your life in a way that will bring glory unto Him.

b. He favours the humble. God normally and naturally favours the humble. If a person is about to enter into trouble, one of the easiest ways of knowing is that such a person begins to get arrogant. But the person who keeps a humble attitude positions himself as a candidate of God's favour. Psalms 25:9 tells us that God guides the humble in judgment and teaches the humble his ways. Jesus Christ, our perfect example, encouraged us to learn from Him because He is meek, gentle and lowly in heart (Matthew 11:29) If any man will be guided by God, his humility index must be very high.

c. Seekers are finders. Jeremiah 29:13 makes it clear that when we seek God and do so with the whole of our heart, we will find Him. This tells us immediately that there is no half-hearted searching of God.

CHAPTER FOUR

THE POWER OF BLESSINGS

Genesis 49:1, 22-26

BLESSING IS A major key that God has handed unto humans and also a veritable way God demonstrates His power among men. I submit to you, dear reader, that there is a wide gap between a person who is blessed and the one who is not blessed. The one who has the key does not need to struggle banging on the door or trying to force his way in; he simply puts in the key and the door opens unto him.

If we are to define blessing, we can simply call it a life force that propels a person into success and victory. A more detailed definition of blessing is "when all the forces in heaven, on earth and underneath the earth are summoned to help a person." What this portends is that a person who is blessed seem to be pushed by unseen hands to the direction he should be headed. The person makes the right decision, takes the right action, meets the right people at the right time, speaks the right words (what other people say and get into trouble, he may say it in a manner that draws applause to him), his little efforts yield great results and even his mistakes turns out to be an innovation.

The people around a blessed man tend to always ask the question – how did you do it? The outcomes defy every known calculation. Sadly, not many people attribute their success to the power of God's blessing, and so they tend to arrogate to themselves the power to become successful.

The people around a blessed man tend to always ask the question – how did you do it? The outcomes defy every known calculation.

The truth of the matter is that blessing cannot be hidden and much more so, it can be 'contagious'. Genesis 30:27, Jacob's uncle, Laban, acknowledged that God had blessed him because of Jacob and on that basis, he persuaded him to stay with him. He declared that he had learned from experience that the blessings he received was as a result of his association with Jacob. It is unfortunate that some people discover very late the associations that could facilitate their blessing. The man Laban was wise enough to know that the things he was getting was not based on his own merit. Association is a major constituent part of the discourse on blessing; good profitable association should be guarded jealously.

Evidence That A Person Is Under The Influence of The Power of Blessing

A person who is under the influence of the power of blessings:

a. ***Makes right decisions and right choices,*** as if he is being guided by some invisible forces even in the most hostile of environments. The example of Joseph comes to mind in this regard, especially during his time in the house of Potiphar. We can talk about his discipline and diligence, but more importantly I believe, the force of blessing was behind the success of Joseph. His father loved him so much that even before he pronounced a blessing on him in Genesis 49, his heart had been blessing him all along. This he showed through physical expressions among which was the adornment with a coat of many colours. No wonder when he was in a difficult situation, he just made the right choice. What about the young David and the decision he faced to either kill or spare King Saul when the opportunity presented itself (I Samuel 24:4-7)? Even when he had "good reasons" to kill the man called Nabal, he eventually made the right decision thanks to the intervention of Abigail. David would have become blood-guilty because of a man who was already inches away death as at the time of his encounter with David. Within ten days after the encounter, Nabal eventually died (I Samuel 25:39). What about Father Abraham? Blessed of the Lord, he had glorious promises hanging over his life; but one great decision to obey God in a rather difficult situation cemented his fatherhood of nations forever. Just let the blessings of God reign over your life, I guarantee you that you will turn in the right direction always, in a way that even you cannot explain. Decision making is what makes our lives, and a blessed person makes the right decision.

b. ***Meets the right people at the right time.*** In truth–a man is only as good as the quality of people released into his life to help him. God has a strategic way of helping men through the ministry of men. It is a clear-cut sign that a man is operating under the influence of the power of blessing, when people rise up to offer him help freely. Sometimes, you can gauge how blessed you are by the team you have, by the quality of people surrounding you. Sometimes, the strength of an enterprise is not necessarily because of the man who is the arrowhead, it is in those flanking him to ensure that his vision is translated into tangible results. Again, taking the example of David, imagine the mighty men that God raised for him, men who were solid in character and diligent in business, men who were risk takers, men who were loyal even to the point of death. Some broke through the camp of the enemies to fetch David the water he desired to drink. On another occasion, one of his aides Abishai rescued David from the attack of a giant when David grew faint in battle – II Samuel 21:15-18).

c. ***Makes little efforts but gets great result.*** For a blessed person, his life is not defined by the level of hard work but by the level of results. This does not mean he is a slacker or a slothful person, but one who shoots with precision and ends up hitting multiple targets.

d. ***Enters into a position of enduring progress.*** There is a world of difference between having a taste of an experience and actually living in that experience. As surreal as it was that a donkey spoke in the Bible, never again was it recorded that that same donkey spoke with the voice of a man (Numbers 22:28).

That was a taste of the experience. A blessed person does not just taste, he lives in it. It is a question of belongingness – a truly blessed person belongs, he is not just a passerby.

e. ***Gets a new name (Genesis 32:24-28).*** The circumstances surrounding Jacob's birth and even his character traits as he grew did not exactly tally with his actual stature as the blessed one. As he progressed in life until he began to raise a family of his own, the power of blessings at work in his life was undeniable. But a time came when the blessing would move to a new level, and the change of gear meant that he would now be known by a new name.

Accessing The Blessing

a. ***Keep your head down.*** Humility is critical when it comes to being blessed. You must bow your heart to be able to be blessed by God because only the humble attracts His grace, He keeps a safe distance from the proud. Also, humble your heart in your relationship with other people, for he who in his own estimation thinks he is better than all around him cannot draw blessings from the people God has placed in his life.

b. ***Trigger the blessing.*** Trigger blessings by the support you provide and the helping hands you lend unto others. Trigger blessings by the atmosphere of peace you create. Ever before the final blessing was pronounced on Joseph by his father, the young man, was well behaved and sharp. This quality all the more endeared him to his father in a way that drove his brothers to jealousy. Even after many years away from home, now as second-in-Command to Pharaoh of Egypt, Joseph still honoured his father. When his father was to come down to Egypt, he sent a chariot to bring his father down. When his father also arrived, he did not wait for his father to come to him, rather he mounted another chariot and went to meet Jacob in Goshen (Genesis 46). No wonder when it got to his turn for the final blessings, Jacob poured out the best of blessings from his heart on Joseph (Genesis 48:15-16). We also should not forget the power of prayers in triggering blessings, like it happened in the experience of Jabez (I Chronicles 4:9-10).

c. ***Hold tight to what you have (because blessings can be lost).*** Revelation 3:11. As previously mentioned, true blessing is enduring. Stay in the place of blessedness. Don't abandon or despise what brought you the blessing in the first place. Eschew self-congratulation. Look down on no one. Fight to keep your blessing by honouring God daily.

Trajectory of The Blessed Life

> *He sent a man before them, even Joseph, who was sold for a servant: Whose feet they hurt with fetters: he was laid in iron: Until the time that his word came: the word of the Lord tried him. The king sent and loosed him; even the ruler of the people, and let him go free.*
> (Psalms 105:17-20)

Humanly speaking, the trajectory of Joseph's life right from the time he had his dreams was a downward spiral, going from one problem to another. He missed being killed by his brothers by just whiskers, and eventually got sold into slavery by the same brothers. Just when he began to settle down in slavery and was building an impressive profile that puts him ahead of other slaves, he landed in prison where probably he had no hope of walking out alive... until something changed!

There are some truths that we tend to overlook but they make a great impact on our destiny, and so it is important that we pay close attention to them.

Truth #1

Everyone on the surface of the earth has a path of travel, sometimes called the trajectory of life. Sadly some people are not sensitive to this truth early enough. Some people have hit the ground before discovering that they had been travelling on a downward path all along, while some are clever enough to do an appraisal mid-way when they begin to observe some patterns. In I Timothy 1:12-13, Paul the Apostle gave an example of how his life was on a downward slope until he had an encounter with the Lord Jesus Christ who changed the trajectory of his life and made a beauty out of him. The greatest change in trajectory that anyone can experience in life is an encounter with Jesus Christ, a change that settles a man's story for all eternity. Aside from the great change in eternal destination, trajectories also change in the ordinary existence of life. The story of Esau also presents a profound example of one who was already down both in the stream of prophecy and in actual manifestation. According to Genesis 25:23, this was the man about whom it was said that he would serve his brother, and according to Genesis 27:3-40, he was the person who got the leftover of blessing after Isaac had generously blessed his younger brother who got the blessing by trickery. Guess what! That leftover blessing was enough for him to keep him from serving his brother. Esau eventually broke free according to his father's admonition, and that changed the trajectory of his life. He grew so strong that when in the future there was going to be a meeting between the two brothers, it was the one who was generously blessed that was now afraid of the one who got the leftover blessing. When Jacob heard that Esau was coming to meet him with 400 men in his company, he feared greatly.

Truth #2

The trajectory of life is changeable through varying degrees of forces. Some people have had their trajectory changed just by a little investment of efforts, some others have had their trajectory changed just through the corrective words and counsels of other men especially authority figures – these are relatable human experiences. But at a deeper level, trajectories do change through encounters like in the case of Peter in Luke 5:1-11 – that encounter was sufficient a force to change the trajectory of his life forever from an ordinary fisherman (maybe successful but nothing more) to a pillar of the church. Conversely and sadly, there are also forces that knock people off the good course they are travelling and before anyone knows what is happening, they are already knocked off track and straight to the ground. This was the experience of Solomon, a man so loved by God but deviated into condoning idolatry. If not for the covenant of mercy that his father, David, received on his behalf, he would have ended terribly. There are cities where things were going well until the force of wickedness crept in and changed their trajectories for the worse. There are organisations that were doing brilliantly well until the force of disunity and misalignment changed the equation. There are homes filled with joy and fruitfulness until conflict and discord changed the trajectory.

Truth #3

The process of change of trajectory is the prerogative of God – He determines and works it out according to His sovereignty. This is because only God holds the power of reversing the irreversible (Luke 1:37, Jeremiah 32:17), and only God holds the access to great and mighty mysteries unknown to man (Jeremiah 33:3). The ultimate power to change the trajectory of a man's life resides with God. Jabez understood this truth when his life was filled with sorrow, leading him to pour out his heart unto the

The process of change of trajectory is the prerogative of God – He determines and works it out according to His sovereignty.

One who holds the power to change the trajectory of a man's life.

CHAPTER FIVE

THE POWER OF CORRECTION

O Lord, I know the way of man is not in himself;
it is not in man who walks to direct his own steps.
O Lord, correct me, but with justice; Not in Your
anger, lest You bring me to nothing.
(Jeremiah 10:23-24, NKJV)

GOD IS NOT shocked about the state of any man. He knows both the internal and external frame of every man as well as the things that are beyond man's awareness and reality. So, when He steps into a man's affairs to make corrections, it is because He has seen what the recipient of His correction has not seen.

Correction is one of the greatest acts of God's mercy available for our good. This explains why one of the greatest admonition ever given was recorded in Proverbs 3:11-12:

Correction is one of the greatest acts of God's mercy available for our good.

My son, do not despise the chastening of the Lord nor detest His corrections. For whom the Lord loves He corrects, just as a father the son in whom he delights.

One of the markers that God is still mindful of a person is correction. It is a dangerous thing for a man to be left alone to his devices.

Seven Points At The Heart Of Correction

The list is not exhaustive, there could be more but these seven points are highlights among many.

1. A good attitude to correction guarantees success.

The greatest determinant of ***success*** is ***attitude***, and the most important attitude that brings success is ***change***. A person with the right attitude to change will be ***teachable***, and you can only be teachable if you are prepared to be ***corrected***. A teachable person is ***humble***.

2. ***Humans need correction because they make mistakes.*** This is simply a reminder that we are not infallible and so we should be careful never to assume we have things perfectly figured out. The best of man is a work in progress. We learnt a vital lesson from the life of the Apostle Paul who showed what it means to be open to correction and the humility to make immediate adjustments.

> *You sit there to judge me according to the law, yet you yourself violate the law by commanding that I be struck!" Those who were standing near Paul said, "How dare you insult God's high priest!" Paul replied, "Brothers, I did not realize that he was the high priest; for it is written: 'Do not speak evil about the ruler* (Acts 23:3-5).

The man was totally wrong to have struck Paul, and humanly speaking, his momentary outburst could even be described as the mildest response that one whose face had just been smacked could give in the circumstance. But Paul was so humble! In one breath, he showed his fallibility as a human being and he admitted it when his attention was called to his error. He did not defend his error neither did he justify it.

3. ***Flinching, recoiling and extreme sense of shame when corrected is a bad sign.***

An extreme sense of shame when corrected is often rooted in pride or sometimes in a perfectionistic temperament. But we must be careful not to take ourselves too seriously, we should be open to correction and learn from our errors with meekness. Don't be defensive. This was the attitude of King Saul when he was corrected by Prophet Samuel in I Samuel 15:30. He was so concerned about his reputation before his people to the point that the mistake mattered little to him compared to his honour.

4. ***Ability and capacity to take corrections are in levels.***

   The greatest test of your attitude to correction is when it is given by your subordinates, because it takes humility to receive correction from the people you have some measure of authority over. But then, there is a further step to this, which is the correction that comes from your contemporaries. If you struggle to take correction from your peers, you need to start praying. And to take it even further, if you cannot take correction from superiors, it is a lost case, except by divine intervention. But God can take us beyond the point where regardless of the quarters the correction is coming from, there is grace to take it. The Bible says that *whoever stubbornly refuses to accept criticism will suddenly be destroyed beyond recovery* (Proverbs 29:1).

5. ***The greatest gift (legacy) for a child is to equip him/her with how to take corrections and criticisms.***

   People are getting more fickle and over-sensitive as the years go by. Teach your wards how to handle corrections and criticisms because inside every criticism, there might be a modicum of valuable life lesson. Even sometimes when criticisms come out of harsh and hostile motives, the ability to take them gracefully toughens a person so that he/ she is not easily broken by the scourge of the tongue. A good deal of wisdom and balance is required in hostile environments we sometimes operate in. The Bible advised us *not to withhold appropriate discipline from a child, it says we should go ahead and punish that child when he needs it, the punishment won't kill him* (Proverbs 23:13). Do not withhold, and do not stop others from contributing to guiding your child.

6. ***It takes great skills to offer corrections that will be well taken.***

The skill to regularly correct others and they take it is a rare gift. God has it in loads and buckets, and He gives it generously to people. There were many seemingly lost cases in the Bible that God fixed through the power of correction. The correction of Peter remains one of the greatest example we can talk about. An overconfident man who assumed he was infallible but got gently corrected through wise words and intercessions by the Master. It takes great skills to correct people and they accept it. This is why correction does not only always stop at the door of the other person, there is need to look inward and ask yourself how you are administering the correction. The Bible in Jeremiah 10:24 tells us that some of the methodology God adopts in administering correction is through mercy and justice, not in anger or hot displeasure. There is an axiom that compares corrections administered in love to dealing a spank with the right hand but cuddling the recipient with the left hand. This is not natural to everyone, it takes a degree of skillfulness to do this. Whatever we do as individuals, we must learn the skill of correcting. There is another well-known saying that balances this point: nobody cares how much you know until they know how much you care. We can possess the skill, but we need God Himself to teach us. So, the onus is on both parties – the person being corrected must respond right, but the person administering

We can possess the skill, but we need God Himself to teach us.

the correction must also get it right by doing it gracefully and graciously.

7. **The art and the skills of taking corrections and criticism are prerequisites for a successful life.** There is an art of taking corrections – we need to seek it, we need to develop it and we need to use it. First, when you are being corrected, calm down and do not be defensive. If whatever is being said to you is right, say 'thank you'; but if it is wrong, humbly go back and explain yourself (don't argue, don't be smug). If the other person is still insisting, though they are wrong, check yourself again–it may not be the substance the person is correcting but your style. You may say or do things as impeccably as possible, but the manner of presentation or body language could be entirely out of order. This explains why it is important to look inward. But if it is neither style nor substance, just move on humbly and never toe the path of quarrel. This is what meekness is, and it is only the meek (the person who has the power to fight back but chose to walk away) that the Bible records will inherit the earth.

This is the guarantee on which the statement is founded that the art and skills of taking corrections and criticism are prerequisite for a successful life.

Reflection

What we have come to know as the gospel is a message of correction, because man had been travelling in the wrong direction until Jesus came in human form to correct our tracks. It therefore makes sense that the eternal destination of every man will be determined by whether or not he heeded the correction of the Lord.

CHAPTER SIX

THE POWER OF GOD'S MIGHTY HANDS

O Lord God of hosts, Who is mighty like You, O Lord? Your faithfulness also surrounds You.

You rule the raging of the sea; when its waves rise, You still them.

You have broken Rahab in pieces, as one who is slain; You have scattered Your enemies with Your mighty arm.

The heavens are Yours, the earth also is Yours; The world and all its fullness, You have founded them.

The north and the south, You have created them; Tabor and Hermon rejoice in Your name.

You have a mighty arm; Strong is Your hand, and high *is Your right hand.*
(Psalms 89:8-13, NKJV)

The greatest human weakness is the inability to fully access and understand the challenges that lie ahead of us. If a lady (for instance) has the faintest idea that this man who is all loving and romantic today may turn out to be abusive in the future, she would have fled for her life. If a man knows that a particular journey will end on a sad note, he definitely would not embark on the journey. I have deliberately painted these pictures because day after day, we are faced with issues that awaken our consciousness to the fact that the best and most instinctual of humans cannot accurately tell what lies ahead.

There are so many things that we do not know, we call them unforeseen circumstances – and as long as we live here on earth, there will always be such events. These things called unforeseen circumstances is by design, God purposely intended it to be like that because only He, the Sovereign One, mysteriously lives outside of time and in time so that the past and future are present before Him. This explains why only God has a solution to all shades and grades of unforeseen circumstances.

The story of Abraham gives us an example of a man who had a lot of unforeseen circumstances to deal with, including leaving his families and embarking on a journey to an unknown destination (Genesis 12:1-3). His nephew became difficult as they journeyed on, and on top of all these, he was hoping for a promised land. The same was true of the disciples of Jesus – 'follow me and I will make you...' (Matthew 4:19) was what He said to them, and they followed to the point where they paused and asked what was in it for them considering that they had left everything just to follow Jesus.

So unforeseen circumstances are not only experienced in our ordinary daily affairs. But even in our deeper spiritual walk with God, there are unforeseen circumstances. And unforeseen circumstances take place to the end that God may show forth His mighty hands.

Victory is only assured in life's battles when God's hand is involved.

Victory is only assured in life's battles when the hand of God is involved. When we talk about some people having the Midas touch, it is important to imagine what it would be like when the hand of God touches our lives and our situations. If God, the Maker of gold and silver, touches a person, we should rest assured that the fellow will immediately become unrecognizable because God's mighty hands command power, the power of transformation. That is why as a matter of advice, when you have struggled and it seems like nothing is working out, ask that the hand of God should come upon you.

Situations and circumstances of life respect the command of God's hand. What this means is that when God lifts His hand, even without a word backing that action, seen and unseen forces come to a standstill. There are countless things that God's mighty hands can accomplish in a man's life, but just to mention a few:

a. ***The hand of God shields from disaster*** (seen, unseen and unforeseen). One of the greatest challenges of life are things that we do not know exist in our space or reality, but they are there lurking in the dark and waiting for the right opportunity to leap upon a man. A number of people are in situations that make them wonder how they landed where they found themselves; but there is a hand that is strong and powerful to save and to shield. It is the strong and mighty hand of the Lord. Psalms 91:4 describes His Wings as a place of refuge and His Truth as a Shield and Buckler. The strong hand of God is man's sure bet for protection that is beyond any known security architecture no matter how robust, nor any financial management scheme no matter how promising.

b. ***The hand of God snatches out of present danger.*** Only God can snatch a person out of the danger that he is already in, like the deep end of dangers such as debt (among many examples). The example of debt comes to mind because this is a generation that is being swallowed up in debt and people are crying for freedom every day because of the weight of the debt. The story of the three Hebrew boys that were delivered from the furnace in Daniel 3:1-27 shows the kind of deliverance the Lord gives when He arises to rescue a man who is currently in danger. This explains why Isaiah 43:2 is a standing promise for those who belong to God, that when you go through the fire it shall not burn you and the flames will not kindle upon you because of His presence and because of His powerful hands holding you.

c. ***The hand of God sends into destiny.*** When God is determined to help a person, nobody can stop that fellow because nobody can stop God. The hand of God can launch a man into his destiny, and there are two ways He can accomplish this – He can pull you into your destiny (like He did with David when he was absent at his own coronation ceremony and God would not let Samuel even sit down until David was brought from the distant place he was at that time – I Samuel 16). By all known physical and strategic criteria for becoming a king, there was no way David was qualified, at least in human estimation, especially when you line him up with his brothers who ticked all the boxes especially with respect to physicality and membership of the nation's army. But God brought David out of obscurity, giving credence to the power of God to pull a man into his destiny regardless of his current location. The second way God can launch a man into his destiny is through a push, and the example that explains this power was also evident in the life of David. The man David was tending his father's sheep in the field – the few sheep as his brother mentioned – and then Jesse his father asked him to go into the field to deliver supplies unto his brothers. To show that God was the One pushing David, his arrival was just-in-time, at the exact time Goliath was roaring his threats (although he had been doing that for 40 days, he wasn't doing it every hour of the day) and the people of Israel were panicky. This sight was what troubled David to the point that he began to ask questions. God's hands pushed him to the point where those who heard him decided to mention him to King Saul. The hand of God kept pushing him a little at a time until he returned with Goliath's head. All David was doing was acting in obedience under God (read I Samuel 17). God pushes us a step at a time and all He expects from us is obedience even when we do not understand what is going on or where the push is leading. The killing of Goliath was the beginning of David's final push into destiny after he had been earlier anointed in the presence of his brothers.

d. The hand of God secures in the place of honour – It is better not to have been a champion than to be a former champion. If Saul had been left as the handsome guy that he was: tall, attractive and responsible family man, a rallying point and significant man in his little community; he probably would have been better off and made a good name for himself within his little sphere of influence. However, he was pushed to be a king, but sadly made a shipwreck of his journey, forgetting that the hand of God that can pull into and push into destiny can also pull back when a man decides to go against God (I Samuel 15:16-23). There is so much metaphorical gravitational force working on everyone who is rising. That is why sustainability is key for anyone aspiring for great heights. There is no joy in sharing stories of good old days, and this is why we need the strong hand of God not just to push us up but to keep us up. We need the hand of God to secure us in our place of grace so that we do not end in disgrace.

We need the hand of God to secure us in our place of grace so that we do not end in disgrace.

That Your Hand Would Be With Me

> *And Jabez was more honourable than his brethren: and his mother called his name Jabez, saying, because I bare him with sorrow. And Jabez called on the God of Israel, saying, Oh that thou wouldest bless me indeed, and enlarge my coast, and that thine hand might be with me, and that thou wouldest keep me from evil, that it may not grieve me! And God granted him that which he requested.* (I Chronicles 4:9-10)

As we go through life, whether flying high or walking on the ground, whether living a honourable life or a struggling life, what you need more than anything else is the hand of God. Jabez recognized this fact and he anchored his prayers on this one important requirement for success – the hand of God.

In a number of life's situations, all we need to make progress is the involvement of the hand of God. This is not just some convenient religious position, it is the truth of all time. Some of such life's situations include:

a. ***When our reality does not match our belief.*** It is a frustrating place to be in life when a person's realities do not match what he believes. Or when what a person has been confessing over time is different from what he is seeing in terms of results and outcomes. This was the position Gideon found himself and the entire nation of Israel at some point, that even when the Angel of the Lord appeared unto him, he was not shy to bear his mind about how the nation's reality didn't match its belief. He said: '... *Oh my Lord, if the Lord* be with us, why then is all this befallen us? And where be all his miracles which our fathers told us of, saying, did not the *Lord* bring us up from Egypt? But now the *Lord* hath forsaken us, and delivered us into the hands of the *Midianites.'* (Judges 6:13).

b. ***When the result we get is not commensurate with the effort we put in.*** This was pretty much the situation in John 21:5-6 when the resurrected Jesus appeared unto His disciples who had toiled fruitlessly for fish until the Lord intervened. This is another situation that makes it evident that the hand of God is a feature that our lives cannot do without. Humanly speaking, when the results are not matching the efforts, the prescription is always to put in more efforts without being discouraged or change strategy; but the earlier anyone realizes that the missing link is the hand of God, the better.

c. ***When you genuinely feel hard done by.*** When life is not fair, complaining will not do. When you feel people who are less capable or less qualified than you are thriving, banging the head against the wall at such moments will not help in any way. When a person finds himself in this situation, the best bet is to cry unto God like the children of Israel did in Exodus 2:23.

d. ***When a person is mocked – by situation or by people.*** There are mockers everywhere, those who for reasons best known to them are waiting to see what becomes of your life, of your investment, of your trust in God, etc. There must have been a conviction in the man called Jabez that there were great expectations from the life of one assumed to be honourable. There was truly honour in him, but situations mocked him. Or shall we speak of David, a king who was humiliated by his own son (Absalom) who executed a coup against his father, causing David to run out of Jerusalem bare-footed. To make matters worse, a man called Shimei from the family of Saul, saw David fleeing and decided to add to the humiliation by hurling stones and curses at him (II Samuel 16:4-14). The sting of that mockery generated doubt in David, who actually resigned to the opinion that he was the architect of his own problems.

From Jabez's Experience – Outcomes of the Hand of the Lord

When the hand of the Lord comes upon a man who has experienced hard life like Jabez, what are the evident outcomes?

a. There will be ***progress*** in place of stagnation. To look longingly at what we desire, and yet have no means of obtaining what we crave for is one of the most demoralizing aspects of life. The hand of God pushes a person in sorrow into joy. Hannah knew nothing but sorrow of heart for many years, until she encountered the God whose hands lifts up and advances into great and glorious places. Hannah was able to sing shortly after she progressed into the status of motherhood, and she said: "He (God) raises the poor from the dust and lifts the beggar from the ash heap to set them among princes and make them inherit the throne of glory..." (1 Samuel 2: 8).

b. There will be ***rapid progress*** in the face of opposition (I Kings 18:45-46). Some movements are only of benefit if they are done swiftly. When the hand of God is upon a person, movement is expedited. Elijah had to get to Jezreel quickly before the rain fell and cause a flash flood. The king did not offer Elijah a seat on his chariot, but having God on his side Elijah was not left stranded. This is a further proof that he is a man who has a standing with God.

The hand of God indeed gives us speed in our lives.

c. ***Inexplicable progress*** amid human limitations. This is where the example of David readily comes to mind again, a man whose path was littered with many limitations beginning with his position and standing in his family. King Saul hated him to the point that he would have pinned David to the wall with his javelin, not on one occasion but many. But the progress David made under the hand of the Lord was an inexplicable one, it was one that even he could not explain.

d. ***Trans-generational progress*** that glorifies God. The ultimate blessing of God on a life, is the blessing that lasts the person's whole life and transfers unto the subsequent generations; often three or four generations down the line. A person that is very much loved by God will enjoy a covenant of perpetual blessing and progress. From Abraham right up to Jacob, it was one long story of trans-generational blessing, until Jacob was accounted as exceedingly rich. A good man leaves an inheritance (legacy in all its expressions) for his children's children (Proverbs 13:22).

CHAPTER SEVEN

THE POWER OF A HEALTHY SOUL

Jeremiah 30:17, III John 1:2

MANY PEOPLE WALK around like wounded lions and sometimes such people do not even know they are hurting and bleeding until something happens that sparks a reaction. At that instance, bystanders will be wondering what has necessitated the reaction, but it has always been there.

The soul of man is often ignored because it is tucked away from sight and from our consciousness. Soul neglect is about the commonest and most

> Soul neglect is about the commonest and most consequential self-abuse that people suffer.

consequential self-abuse that people suffer from. Our Lord Jesus Christ pointed to the fact that men have the tendency to go after material things with greater attention and dedication, but eventually neglect the wellbeing of the soul. He said in Matthew 16:26 that what shall it profit a man if he gains the whole world but loses his own soul? Remember the man in Luke12:15 who Jesus pointed his attention to how his soul should be a priority rather than the abundance of possessions that he was so much obsessed with.

Unfortunately, having made the above introduction, the neglect of the soul is even made more difficult because not only is it that we do not know where the soul resides, the soul is even more difficult to define. This is one very compounding fact about the soul. Speaking of definition, there are about six main words used interchangeably between the Bible's Old and New Testaments to refer to the soul.

The first is ***Psuche*** which is of Greek origin. It is from this root that the word 'psyche' came to describe the psychology and the inner working of the mind of man. This was a fairly consistent expression of what the soul meant or represented in the Old Testament. The second word which had Hebrew and Aramaic origin is ***Nephesh***, which some have argued is difficult to define in English because the Hebrews do not look at the body and the spirit and the mind the way we ordinarily look at them. Rather, they divided things into what is not seen (Nephesh) and what is seen (Shem). There are two other words that we tend to confuse, which are ***Ruach*** (Hebrew origin meaning spirit) and ***Pneuma*** (Greek origin meaning breath). The focus here is the soul which is that inward part of a person that directs the total wellbeing and real essence of the person. The soul is the inward part of you that must be healthy. It is the inner part that basically directs the external part–the visage that everyone else sees.

Causes Of Soul Sickness And Injury (Causative Factors)

A soul that is not cared for or one that is left unprotected falls sick or becomes wounded. That is why you must be careful not to allow the things seen around you or said about you to hit you so hard to the point of inflicting injuries to your soul. There must be a protection for your soul. Personally, I have a habit of praying daily for deliverance from the scourge of the tongue. It is your duty to care for your soul so that you don't walk around with wounds that will adversely affect the trajectory of your life.

It is your duty to care for your soul and feed your soul always, doing all things possible to ensure that your soul does not get shriveled and malnourished. Even a whole and robust soul needs constant guarding because someone can shoot an arrow at it and it begins to bleed instantly (Psalms 109:22, Job 5:21, Psalms 31:20, Psalms 57:4, I Kings 19:1-4, Matthew 11:28-29, Isaiah 6:5, Proverbs 21:8).

So, what are the causes of soul sickness and injury?

1. **Words**

   People need to be very careful with their choice of words so they do not cause harm to others. May I advise that you do not pride yourself in ***saying your mind*** but rather ***mind what you say***. This is because it is easy to say what is on your mind but it is difficult or even impossible to take it back. No matter how much we try to shrug it off, words are powerful and many people have not recovered from the effects of words directed at them. Words are powerful, it is not in vain that the whole essence of God is called 'The Word'.

2. **Difficult life experiences.**

   Difficult life experiences can also cause soul sickness and injury. An example is hope deferred which the Bible says makes the heart sick (Proverbs 13:12) and the person may not even be aware that he has been wounded by the delay or unmet expectation. Bereavement can also wound a person in a way that recovery becomes very difficult and just a little trigger will peel open the emotional expression that accompanies the wound. But no matter how difficult your experience is, God is able to restore health to you and heal your wounds. You must only be careful not to allow those difficult situations define you, and be even more careful not to draw dangerous and negative conclusions from those experiences. For instance, some people have said things like 'I will never be the same again'. It is important that we do not compound issues with such words. The reason I am averse to such confession is because I believe in God's ability to restore wounded souls (Psalms 23:3).

3. Sin

What sin does is that it defaces us and brings guilt, and what guilt does is that a person is no longer free to be who he/she ought to be. That is why if there is any sin in your life, quickly bring it under the blood of Jesus for perfect cleansing and liberation. Sin lingers! There are details in our past that we are not able to talk about because of the wounding of sin. For some people, because of the life they had lived in the distant past, they tend to get very defensive when discussions about chastity or any other virtue comes up. But for as long as you have brought it under the cover of the blood of Jesus, you are no longer the old person. After God healed Paul, he never dwelt on his past again. This explains why he was able to say if any man is in Christ, he is a new creature.

4. Isolation

Because the soul is the living part of you, it gets refreshed by stimulation. This is why if you raise a child without stimulation, the child will not thrive. Every part of a child's development comes with stimulation. The same thing applies to the soul of a man; it is the baby inside of you and must be stimulated by things around. This explains why even Elijah, as anointed as he was, when he became isolated, he sank so low that he was wishing for death (I Kings 19:4). The only perfect human that ever lived, the man Jesus, was never at any point isolated – He loved and lived a communal life. Let us be wary of isolation because it wounds the soul in a very unpleasant way. It is an avenue of keeping the wound open and fresh.

5. Environment

Environment can be a source of injury to the soul, especially the kind of environment that we have come to know as a 'toxic environment'. Some environments could be so toxic that 24 hours is a long time for a person to be gravely impacted. Some people never swore until they found themselves in an environment, some people do not grumble or murmur until they found themselves in an environment, some people were law abiding until they were part of an environment where there is breakdown of law and order. As a matter of fact, it gets to a point that even the body begins to rebel against the negative influence of the environment. This explains why (spiritually speaking) it is important to always fumigate your environment by praying always in the Spirit so that the spiritual viruses

> Detoxify your environment so that you do not get sick or get wounded.

resident in an environment will not infect your soul. Detoxify your environment so that you do not get sick or get wounded in your soul.

6. **Lack of rest/weariness.**
   Do you know that physical exercise does not make us to be as tired as inward stress? Inner stress is the worst kind of stress a man can experience and we must know or find a way of resting our minds.

Evidence of Soul Sickness

Some of the telltale signs of a sick, wounded soul are:

1. **Timidity**
   We saw this in the life of Timothy, and this was why the Apostle Paul admonished him in II Timothy 1:7 that he had not be given the spirit of fear but of power and of love and of sound mind. We could say that Timothy's soul was not so whole because of the attacks he had endured. How did we know this? Remember Paul had earlier admonished him

pointedly in I Timothy 4:12 not to allow anyone intimidate him or despise him because he was a youth. He said: *Let no one despise you for your youth, but set the believers an example in speech, in conduct, in love, in faith, in purity*. Paul's admonition to Timothy immediately tells us that we only fight attacks on our souls by the knowledge of who we are. The attacks on Timothy probably affected him so much to the point that he developed stomach problems which could be attributed to stress among other causes (I Timothy 5:23). All these began by the despising of men, which got to Timothy's soul and birthed timidity, and the external effect was physical ailment. It is never a good sign for you to find yourself looking down always. It is not a good sign when you enter into a room and immediately begin to feel like you do not measure up. When these things happen, no matter the amount of a bold face that you put up, you definitely need the help of God for a healthy soul. Public speaking, for instance, can be very hard. In fact there is no one person alive that does not have some trepidations about public speaking; but when it becomes so difficult that even among a small circle of friends you are tongue-tied, you may need to examine yourself to see if something is holding you back in the soul. These are little indicators people must consciously and prayerfully look out for before they become bigger.

2. **Paranoia**

Paranoia was the undoing of Saul, Israel's first anointed king. Such a sad episode. In fact, the latter end of his life was characterised by severe paranoia. In the event in I Samuel 18:7 where the women of the city sang and ascribed a thousand to Saul and ten thousand to David, a man with a sound mind would have reveled in the chant and probably say something like – 'that's my boy!'. But rather, Saul only grew jealous and angry. This is a lesson for those who hold position of authority – are you one who cannot stand a subordinate outshining you even if it is momentarily? Watch it. Even after the chants, the young man David still acknowledged and respected Saul's authority, he continued to call him 'father'. Imagine if Saul had not allowed paranoia to have the better of him, how much greater honour he would have received. We must admit that we are living in incredible times when people are rising up to do great things, some of whom we have some degree of advantage or authority over. It takes a sound mind not to be threatened by the successes of these protégés and not to try to take the glory for the exploits they are doing. Embrace them with genuine love in your heart and the joy of seeing an 'offspring' grow. By the time we got to I Samuel 22:11-18, Saul's paranoia led him to kill about 85 priests, who according to him, conspired against him by giving a starving David bread and inquiring of God for him. What an evil man! We must be very careful to not assume that we are incapable of such wickedness – jealousy has no limit, and no man who has that tendency knows what he is capable or incapable of doing. Right from wishing people bad to even turning your eyes away from something that can hurt another person, an unwholesome soul just does not have a limit to the evil it is capable of.

3. Instability and vacillation

This is about the commonest evidence of a sick soul. For some people, making decision is never an easy adventure – they think through and through, yet never get to make a decision, or end up making the worst of decisions. A healthy soul is not afraid to make decisions. Of course the carefulness that should go with the decision-making will be ensured, but he is open to accept the outcome of his decision and make revisions where necessary. Even if it is not revisable, a healthy soul makes up his mind that the impact of the decision will not crush him. The Bible in James 1:6-8 tells us that instability does not only have physical and psychological implications, but also has a spiritual implication, to the extent that an unstable person cannot receive anything from the Lord. One of the challenges Elijah had with the people of Israel in his days was their instability and vacillation (I Kings 18:12). These were people who were halting between two opinions, claiming devotion to God and courting the idol called Baal-Peor in the same breath. Sitting on the fence makes a man get hit on both side. That is the danger of indecision.

4. **Unbridled anger**

When a person loses it completely, it is an evidence of a sick soul. Proverbs 19:11 says *the discretion of a man makes him slow to anger and his glory is to overlook a transgression.* A man of sound mind will not be quick to anger. When everything irritates you, it is an evidence that all is not alright in the soul. The first area a person loses control is in the expression of displeasure at what he does not like, or what is not going his way. The capacity to reject what we do not like and embrace what is good for us, is a survival mechanism that the good Lord has placed in everyone of us. In the physical body, the ability to fight foreign 'invaders' like viruses and bacteria are integral to keeping us healthy. But this immune system must be moderated, or else it can become counterproductive when the fight is now so ferocious that the good cells of the body are also rejected, fought and consumed. When this happens, we talk of autoimmune reactions, which in essence is a disease. So it is with our souls, when the 'good' anger becomes so toxic to the extent that a person is consumed with rage that practically eats away at the emotional wellbeing, then a diseased state of the soul has taken hold. The Bible makes it clear that anger rests in the bosom of fools (Ecclesiastes 7:9), and admonishes that a person should not let the sun go down on his/her wrath (Ephesians 4:26). Please do a regular personal check-up on yourself. At the first sign of unbridled anger, please present yourself to the Great Physician, and He will help you.

5. Moodiness

> Psalms 42:5 says: *why are you cast down O my soul? And why are you disquieted within me? Hope in God, for I shall yet praise Him for the help of His countenance.*

Persistent moodiness is a sign that your soul is sick. Spiritual and emotional asthenia is real. Again, we know all is not well physically when we feel weak and unable to do what we would normally do with ease. The soul also reacts to its ill state by shutting down. Because it is not willing to take on more activities, so as to preserve its sanity, the soul shuts down all activities and this manifests as low mood. A low mood expresses itself in various ways. It can start as just being moody, and can progress all the way to being depressed with all the dangerous outshoot like self-harm. My prayer is that every soul that is cast down shall be lifted by the power of God. Amen.

Maintaining A Healthy Soul

Some interventions for physical illness will not take place unless the patient signs up for some after-operation disciplines. So it is in the things of the soul. So, to thrive, the soul requires the following:

1. **Attention** – You must pay careful attention to your soul. Proverbs 4:23 says keep your heart with all diligence for out of it are the issues of life. Pay attention to the wellbeing of your soul. Don't just go out making a living, go out guarding your soul so that you can enjoy your labour with peace and joy.

2. **Anchor** – Every soul needs an anchor, else it will be heading in different directions in an unstable manner. But there are different things you can anchor your soul on, but the truth is that there is only One that you can anchor your soul on with the guarantee that it will be kept safe and secure. Only GOD should be the anchor for your soul, every other thing you tether your soul unto can be a source of problem. This is not just some convenient Biblical position, it is reality. Anyone who chooses to anchor his soul on riches, on family, should be aware that these things are unstable and therefore such a person's mind is likely to go adrift and become unstable. Love your family, guard your relationships jealously, but do not anchor your soul on relationships because the day the relationship shakes, your soul will also be shaken. Anchor your soul to God alone. Aside from the fact that God can restore whatever is lost, He is the only One who is STABLE. This is why it seems believers are happier because they have the right Anchor. The lyrics of an evangelical song says it all:

We have an Anchor that keeps the soul,
Steadfast and sure whilst the billows roll,
Fastened to the Rock which cannot move,
Grounded firm and deep in the Saviour's love.

It is all about Jesus. And this is not a convenient church speak, it is reality. When things do not work out, just hand them over to Jesus and watch Him keep your soul intact.

3. **Attitudes** – You must have some attitudes in your arsenal, and one of such attitudes that will help you maintain a healthy soul is ***hope.*** For people who have lost hope, no matter the level of physical treatment they give them, they still go down. It has been noted in many medical publications that the moment a person with a life-threatening illness decides to die, he/she cannot be stopped. There are some others who just by maintaining hope have prolonged their lives. Another helpful attitude for a healthy soul is gratitude. Those who are grateful

Those who are grateful live better and healthier lives...

live better and healthier lives, and gratitude does not have to be for the big things of lives but even for the things that are seemingly small.

4. **Acceptance** – The soul requires acceptance and acceptance is only received when you give it. Many people are where they are because of rejection. This places a demand on us to do whatever it takes to make those around us feel accepted and appreciated. Please, do not give any vibe of rejection and resentment to anyone. Children particularly have a way of testing whether or not they are accepted, especially on occasions when they are afraid to come home and quacking in their mind because of the perceived judgment that will greet their actions. Before you start dishing out discipline, embrace them. We ourselves were accepted in the beloved in Christ Jesus (Ephesians 1:6). So, we should also give acceptance.

5. **Affirmation (blessings)** – The soul is subject or responsive to two main things throughout life: blessings and curses. It is from the soul that we

curse and it is from the soul that we bless. An example that comes to mind was when Isaac wanted to bless his favoured son, Esau; he gave him an instruction to prepare a special meal for him so that his soul could bless the lad before his death (Genesis 27:4). The soul of man is more powerful than anyone thinks and that explains why a curse may not necessarily be spoken, but a deep sigh from an injured soul could be a game changer. The counsel is that you should be careful not to put yourself in a position where someone's action affects you so terribly that your soul will curse such a person. The flip side is that you should be careful not to put yourself in harm's way. Make sure blessings flow from you always and put yourself in a position where blessings can flow to you from the souls of people you come in contact with.

Treatment For The Soul

The Lord Is Our Healer. There is healing in no other name but in the name of Jesus. It is unto Him we must run. It is by His body and His blood that we are made whole. I know there are other treatments for the soul that we can talk about, like going for counselling, going for many forms of therapy, and so on. We are aware of these other resources, but there is absolutely nothing that can sideline the reality that the Lord is our Healer (Psalms 103:2-4, Exodus 15:26, Isaiah 53:5, Jeremiah 30:17).

CHAPTER EIGHT

THE POWER OF A RENEWED MIND

Romans 12:1-2

A PERSON MAY have the Spirit of Christ but not the mind of Christ in any tangible manner. This is the situation when we see some people who we can say are born again but they have quite some character traits that are concerning. For instance, born again but quarrelsome, proud or slanderous. It is possible some of us have looked at some of these people in the past and concluded that they are not born again because of the manifestation of these traits. As a matter of fact, when we are the ones caught in this kind of situation, we doubt ourselves and ask questions about why some unpleasant traits are still present in our lives.

This has continued to be debated in the Church, especially because the Bible admonishes that if any man is in Christ, he is a new creature; old things have passed away and all things have become new (II Corinthians 5:17). But if we pay close attention to Romans 7, Apostle Paul made some important differentiation between the desire of the Spirit and the eventual act of the person. One thing is sure – we all at one point or another in our lives will be faced with this conundrum because the Spirit indeed may have Christ sitting on its throne, but there is still ongoing work to be done on the mind.

The hallmark is that do you have the witness in your Spirit that you are a child of God? If you have a witness in your Spirit, you need to prayerfully and consciously work on the contradictions that are evident in your life so that the Spirit of God can make your mind to conform to the image of Christ. The Spirit must dictate to the mind, let the mind know that it should submit, and the mind in turn must dictate to the body to submit to the will of the Spirit. That is the order.

The regeneration of the Spirit is the crux of the matter – and this explains why a person can be moral and still go to hell because the spirit of such a man has not received Christ. The differentiation is the witness on the inside that you belong to Him, and it is the continual work of the Lord that caters for the mind.

The spirit and mind do not seem to be unified and there is nothing that could be more troubling for most believers than this fact. Even the Apostle Paul had to cry out: *O wretched man that I am, who shall deliver me from this body of sin?* (Romans 7:24). That contradiction can be so deep in some people that they practically give up walking the Christian way, but if you still have that witness crying within you, it is a matter of prayerful determination to get to your destination.

Another important point with respect to the interaction between the spirit and the mind is a dissonance between profession and possession.

This happens when there are no evidences to back up the confessions we make, but most times when this happens, the challenge is not with the profession but with the mind not agreeing with the spirit to make the profession bring forth fruits.

The understanding of this truth is one of the most important determinants of a healthy relationship both with God and with man.

The Programmed Mind

The mind is programmed to respond promptly to situations, or else a person may be caught in a web of problems as a result of the inability to produce instant answers. God has made it that our mind can respond to external stimuli without sometimes even thinking, and that is why the real person sometimes show up.

This appears to me more like a computing script, a set of instructions that executes when it is invoked especially by another computer programme. So, our minds work like scripts sometimes. When a stimulus comes from without and because we have been programmed in a particular way, we notice that our response follows a sequence like we have been programmed. For instance, anyone who is given to anger, the first time he/she comes across a threatening situation, there will be something rising on the inside; and if nothing interrupts and intercepts the process, you will discover that the person's face begins to change. If that process does not get interrupted, the nose may flare, the ears may move, the face may be flushed, the person may begin to grunt, then he may begin to talk loud and fast, and finally may become physically violent. There is likely nothing that will stop the person from reacting in that sequence except you re-programme that person.

> ...Having an understanding of how the mind works is a necessary step towards a re-engineering of the mind through the help of God.

A person that is fearful as well, once you touch that aspect of the person's life, everything starts moving along the line of fear and before you know what is happening the person might even slide into what is called a panic attack. So, having an understanding of how the mind works is a necessary step towards a re-engineering of the mind through the help of God. We get programmed through our nature (our adamic nature–some of us are born that way), through the experiences of life (similitude of past events) and even through associations, among others.

We get programmed in life to fit two main types of outcomes: first is the way of the world, and the other type of outcome is the way of the Lord.

The Way of The World

The ways of the world are thoughts and patterns that inform our actions. Some of these thoughts and patterns include:

a. **The law of majority** – The law of majority assumes that if something is happening to a large number of people, it invariably means that it may happen to you; or more commonly, if a large number of people subscribe to something, it most probably may be good or the right thing to do. Another name for it is ***the bandwagon effect***. The devil uses this strategy a lot to multiply toxicity in an environment. For example, if there is a gossip about a person, the devil makes sure that the gossip is multiplied until it gets to the point where people begin to believe that there are some elements of truth in the story. That is the way of the world and kingdom people must be careful because many have lost good things in life because other people decided to jump on the bandwagon to slander them. Remember Exodus 23:2 warned us to refrain from joining the multitude to do evil. "Many" does not mean "right". As believers, we are meant to stand out of the crowd, just like God testified that Caleb had a different spirit in Numbers 14:24. This is even more important today because day-by-day, many things that were abnormal before have become normalized, many things that people wouldn't normally talk about let alone do them are becoming entrenched now. These happen because the media and the people who had taken a stand before are beginning to dilly-dally on their stand. This is a very dangerous path to take and it is an evidence of a mind that is yet to be renewed. The responsibility is ours to find out the mind of God and follow the mind of God, not popular opinions and practices. We need to be careful not to normalize what is common.

> ...There are many people that appear very rich but in actual fact are very poor; but on the contrary, there are many who appear very poor but are very rich.

b. Trust your eyes. Seeing is believing. Be careful when people start saying to you "let us face reality", and be more careful not to engage that expression in your conversations because you are indirectly saying "let us ditch faith". That is the way of the world and it is antithetical to the way of the Lord which says *blessed is he who believes without seeing* (John 20:29). It is tough, but that is the way of the Lord. When people say seeing is believing, they forget that the world has a great share of illusions. Seeing should not always inspire our ability to believe, because there are many people that appear very rich but in actual fact are very poor; but on the contrary, there are many who appear very poor but are very rich. We must be careful not to play to the gallery, but be sure that there is more in us than people see. This was the pattern our Lord Jesus Christ lived by when he walked on the earth. Despite being among the people, they saw a new dimension to His person and the depth of His wisdom each passing day. This is what it means to be a person of substance. A person of substance does not run his life based on the premise of the visible, but he lives from the outflow of the abundance on the inside.

c. **If it looks good, feels good and tastes good, then it is definitely good**. This ideology is the foundation of the world's problem. The forbidden fruit looked good to Eve, it was desirous to make a person wise, and then it tasted good also (Genesis 3:6). I John 2:15-16 concluded that everything that is in the world, the lust of the flesh, the lust of the eyes and the pride of life, are not of the Father but of the world. Lust of the flesh is the taste, lust of the eyes is the look and the pride of life is the feeling, and on these three areas, we shall face challenges everyday but we must ride above them. It may feel good but it may not be good, it may smell nice but there may be stench inside of it (May we not purchase dead commodities that have been scented). We must be careful not to allow the world define for us what we accept or embrace as good.

d. **Your own needs take precedence over everything else**. This is what we call self-centeredness or selfishness. The strongest message of the world to us is that we come first in every matter, therefore our concerns should take precedence over those of others. For a balance, it is important to mention that this is not an advocacy to empower others to the detriment of your own wellbeing, but at the same time, it is important to remember that life is not always about you. If it is, then you become narcissistic, thinking the world revolves around you. This is what happens to the one we now address as Satan today, and sadly, we are beginning to raise a world where the virtues of altruism and charity are fast becoming alien to individuals. We are setting the world up for chaos with the "me only" attitude. The Son of God gave His life for the world and there is an addendum to it: that we also need to lay our lives for the brethren just in the fashion He has done for us (I John 3:16). People who live their lives for themselves alone do not always have enough (in their own estimation), so they have to struggle endlessly to acquire more. Romans 12:10 admonishes us to *be kindly affectionate towards one another, giving preference to one another in honour*.

Being transformed to the Lord's way

The process of renewing our minds include the following:

a. **Recognize** that ultimately, the old way is not to your advantage. The way of the world may look okay, it may look like people are treading the path and getting away with it, but you must settle it in your mind that it is not to your advantage. Just watch people who travel that path carefully, if they do not land themselves into trouble, they are actively spoiling others and setting them up for trouble, including their offspring. Those who have sick souls can affect and infect those who hang around them. Remember Proverbs 14:12, *there is a way that seems right to a man, but the end of it is destruction.*

b. Resent the old way. Most times, we do not hate what we do not want enough for us to receive what we love. So, we need to hate what we do not want so much so that we can have the capacity to receive what we love. This was the message the Lord Jesus Christ was passing across in Luke 14:26, that there should be sufficient resentment for the things we do not want. It must get to the point where we can actually feel so sick about the things we do not want in our lives, that we are driven to pray with deep groaning unto the Father. We cannot stop at any stage trying to tolerate the things that are unhealthy for our minds. Colossians 3:8-10 actually captures it as putting off the old man with its deeds, and then putting on the new man which is renewed in knowledge and fashioned after Christ's image.

c. **Recruit** new thoughts and new ways. Recruitment takes time, it takes training and it takes resources. The Word of God is the primary means whereby our minds are renewed. The Psalmist in Psalms 63:6 talks about how he recruited the art of meditation on God and His word as a critical step in renewing his mind. Philippians 4:8 also admonishes that we set our minds on things that are true, things that are honest, things that are noble, things that are just, things that are pure, things that are lovely, things that are of good report, things that are virtuous and praiseworthy.

d. **Retain** and constantly **Refire** the new way. This is the counsel the Apostle Paul gave to Timothy, charging him to meditate on the (good) things and give himself entirely to them so that his progress may become evident to all. The more we meditate on the things that are beneficial for our souls, the better for us.

The ways and customs of the world cannot please the Lord. The needed transformation in our lives will require commitment, consecration and reliance on the Spirit of truth to help us. A renewed mind brings healing to the soul and the body. May we find grace to please the Lord in all things. Amen.